Alyeska's Axioms for Parents

Child-Rearing Wisdom from My Dog

By

Joyce Meagher, RN, LPC, LMFT, RPT-S

Alyeska's Axioms for Parents: Child-rearing Wisdom from my Dog

Published By: LifeSpan Counseling
             kdknzlr@comcast.net

Book Design and Graphics by: JJM Design and Graphics

Printed in the United States

Disclaimer:

ISBN: 978-0-9847150-0-8

Alyeska Definition: "The archaic spelling of the Aleut word Alaska meaning "mainland," "great country," or "great land." – Wikipedia

In Remembrance

…of my beloved St. Bernard, Alyeska, and all the wise lessons she taught me. She was born a very old soul.

Acknowledgements

Deep thanks to Jim Meagher for illustrating and proofreading this book.

Thanks to these additional people for their general comments and help in proofreading:

Mary Chisholm   Holly Erwin   Meredith Gelman   Dee Rushforth

Alyeska's Axioms Table of Contents

1: Remember the unadulterated glee of that first moment you laid eyes on me. ....**Page 2**

2: Enjoy my playful behavior, while setting limits to rein me in safely. .... **Page 6**

3: Give me a healthy diet, and only minimal "dessert," and always after I finish my meals first. I will win if you are inconsistent! **Page 10**

4: When I disobey, teach me what I SHOULD do instead; give me consequences of my behavior calmly. ....**Page 14**

5: Give me freedom to follow my instincts and grow into the adult I'm supposed to become. Praise me when I do a kind act and practice empathy for others! .... **Page 18**

6: Teach me to socialize gently and slowly, without overdoing it or pressuring me. .**Page22**

7: Please notice me when I want or need extra attention or loving.   ....**Page 26**

8: Take time to be extra kind when you need to leave me behind.   ....**Page 30**

9: Please help me when I am helpless. . **Page 34**

10: Continue to love others the way you loved me. I know you have plenty of love to go around. ....**Page 38**

Forward

In reflecting back on last year's loss of my beloved Saint Bernard, Alyeska ("Aly"), I saw many parallels in her training, and resulting behaviors, to that of raising children. As friends and family recalled the kindness and wisdom Aly emanated, an idea emerged to me, as a therapist, to use these memories to write a short, playful book to demystify child-rearing issues for parents.

As a parent, and as a long-term child and family counselor, I am struck by the tedium of many parenting books I've read. Often, the message is lost in the delivery. My clients' parents struggle to get through these books quickly, so as to use the information during the therapy process.

Throughout years of pediatric, emergency room and psychiatric nursing, I observed conflicts in parenting styles that remained evident when I enlarged my career path to become a counselor, specializing in play therapy and teaching parenting techniques to client caregivers.

As parents struggle with the difficulties of child-rearing, common behaviors can emerge in their children from feelings of loss, lack of control or safety, neglect, jealousy, inadequacy and discouragement. Such behaviors include: Disobedience, tantrums, aggressiveness, complaints of negative self-esteem, anxieties, socialization problems, eating problems, difficulty expressing feelings and adjustment problems to environmental changes.

Children change our lives forever. Methods of parenting our children affect them for their entire lifetimes, as does our treatment of our pets. My wish is that this book will give you a little more wisdom, and several easy techniques, to aid you on your journey to becoming more satisfied parents.

Introduction

"Life affords no greater responsibility, no greater privilege, than the raising of the next generation."

- C. Everett Koop

This book contains ten child-rearing axioms, or universal truths, which Aly will walk you through. I believe they are core tenets for successful parenting. My professional and personal experience suggests that parents follow these axioms to alleviate struggles, and to teach their children responsibility and independence.

Each axiom has four sections: A lesson posed by Aly; theoretical and practical discussion by the author; conclusions to consider; and contemplative questions, with space for personal notes.

This book has several purposes:

(1) To help parents quickly digest core concepts significant to positive child-rearing,

(2) To give individual child/family therapists a succinct, organized tool to enable discussion of child-rearing concepts with their individual adult clients,

(3) For group therapists to provide as a workbook to each participant in a multi-session parenting support group. This workbook encourages a structured approach for discussing parenting issues, by focusing on one-to-two axioms per session.

Whatever your purpose, come start your walk with Aly..........

Axiom 1: Remember the unadulterated glee
of that first moment you laid eyes on me.

I remember the day I first came to you: You met me at the airport freight department. I had been enclosed in my little travel pen for what seemed forever, waiting to lay eyes on you. You wore your most festive "expectant parent" St. Bernard gear, including shirt, wristwatch and backpack (given as a Christmas gift years before by your family). You had all ready named me "Alyeska," because you were in Alaska when I was born in the Pacific Northwest.

Your anticipation, after waiting 23 years for another St. Bernard, kept you awake most the night. I tried to relax in my crate on the plane, but wished for a release from the confinement. I knew my life and yours would be forever changed when we met.

I exited from that dark, tiny, crowded crate and staggered with a plop onto the grass, looking expectantly into your eyes. The bright light was blinding, but when I looked at you, your face told me you were hooked forever. The overwhelming love I felt from you was instantaneous, and I knew you planned to take care of me always.

Remember when you awaited your child during that long, nine-month experience? You imagined how your baby would look, how it would act, how you would act as a new parent? You had discussed names together and, finally, had one reserved in anticipation of its birth. Most of all, do you remember the first moment you laid eyes on your child and held him or her in your arms? Recall the thrill, the glee, the momentousness of the occasion. Remember the hundreds of pictures you took (most likely, with a new camera)?

When you feel worn out, discouraged and overwhelmed as a parent, remember those first moments! Always let that protective, unadulterated love shine forth and overpower anything unkind you are thinking of saying in anger to your child. Instead, leave the room for your OWN "timeout" to cool down.

Disciplining while angry is rarely helpful. Of course, there will be safety moments when your reactions must be swift and your voice must be sharp, as when quickly stopping your child from touching a hot stove or from running out into the street without looking. These reactions should be infrequent, and memorable for your child, to drive home the point.

If your child loses control and is unable to calm down, quietly (while YOU still have self-control) give your child a timeout isolated from you (so as to avoid giving secondary gains from negative attention); usually, the child's age in minutes is a good length of time.

When first teaching the timeout process, explain that the child can leave the timeout only once the timer has gone off and if self-control has returned. Do NOT engage with your child if you hear angry screaming or threats. Silently return your child to the timeout area if necessary, but do so dispassionately; restart the timer.

CONCLUSIONS

Words said in anger can be forgiven, but rarely are they forgotten. I have counseled countless children (and adults) who bear the scars of parental comments made in anger, such as: "I wish you'd never been born!" or "You're a BAD child!" or "I'd give anything to get away from you for awhile!!" The results of such comments on self-esteem can be the creation of a negative self- belief such as, "I'm not good enough," or "I'm not loveable."

Instead, state, "I always love you, but RIGHT NOW, I am VERY upset with your behavior!" Then, proceed with the timeout as explained earlier. Once the timeout is over, move on to other activities. Avoid discussion of the incident any further, unless the child requests a deeper understanding of why the timeout occurred; believe me, it's typically obvious to all parties concerned!

Separate your reaction to your child's negative actions from your unconditional love for your child. Always hold IN sight the love you felt at FIRST sight!

1. How does my child know, every day, that I love him or her unconditionally?

2. How do I separate my child's frustrating actions from that unconditional love?

3. What can I do more of in this area?

4. What can I do less of in this area?

NOTES

Axiom 2: Enjoy my playful behavior, while setting limits to rein me in safely.

I really think the cat did that

You laughed at my antics, as I adjusted to my changed environment, tested the boundaries, and gave you affection and love, as readily as you gave them to me.

You knew I would grow rapidly and need rules, so you taught me to sit, lay down, stay and come, all the while giving me consistent praise and attention. I WANTED to obey you, because your praise made me feel happy.

You learned to ignore my attempts to "be leader of the pack," because YOU were the grownup and made the rules! You couldn't help smirking at times when I tried new ways to manipulate those rules, but you knew that any weakness you showed would just egg me on to try again!

Sorry about the slippers... not!

I cannot overemphasize the need for parents to keep rules and limits consistent for their children! Most negative acting-out results when children see loopholes as worth pursuing. Imagine a child being at a playground that is surrounded by a brick wall. If the bricks are solidly-mortared and intact, the child is not stimulated to "test" the solidity of the wall, and instead, just enjoys playing. If there is a loose brick, the challenge can become to "poke" it and see if it gets looser, or falls out. Logic follows that, if one brick were loose, maybe more are! Now, the child is diverted from a focus on enjoyable play, to testing the "limits" of security and strength of that brick wall. Please, minimize the opportunities for your child's acting-out by keeping both the physical and emotional environment simple, safe and predictable.

A major parenting complaint I've heard for years is: "I have to tell him/her ____ times (you fill in the quantity) before he/she listens!!" Imagine just settling in to read the paper while your children are watching television in another room nearby. Suddenly, you hear a ruckus and start repeatedly yelling at them to stop fighting. When parents continue to talk AT children (I call this

"armchair parenting"), instead of responding quickly TO non-compliant children, the children's motivation to respond diminishes accordingly. You finally get up and go deal with the children, but, most probably, in a no-longer calm manner!

So, to keep things manageable: (1) Make a request of your children (you can just say your children's names and see if you get a response; why bother to continue if that doesn't occur?); (2) Clarify that you were understood (have them repeat the request); and (3) React calmly to non-compliance by stopping it!

This response involves getting up, physically turning off the television that is mesmerizing your children, and sending your children to a timeout together until they can arrive at a sharing compromise. In other situations of non-compliance, it can mean removing the spellbinding electronic game from your child's hands (maybe even before starting to talk with them again!). If you observe fighting outside that is distracting your child from responding to you, quietly approach your child to tell him/her to come inside for a room timeout. When out in public, give an immediate consequence that is logical for the situation, such as leaving the restaurant when your child ignores your warning to stop misbehaving.

CONCLUSIONS

"Proactive parenting" is the key!!

Is it frustrating and more wearing initially for you to stop what you are doing to go find, stop or limit your child? Yes, absolutely!

Is it disappointing to have to leave a restaurant? Yes, absolutely!

Is it easier to be inconvenienced once now, than a hundred times in the future, about the same issue? Yes, absolutely!!

Accepting inconvenience as normal is the key to successful parenting! Pro-active parenting helps you raise well-socialized, competent and independent children. It involves encouraging your child calmly, and kindly allowing for mistakes, but remaining firm about your expectations of behavior. Each day and age brings new challenges. Why stay stuck on old issues? There will plenty of future surprises to keep you busy enough as a parent!

QUESTIONS TO PONDER

1. When and where am I comfortable with the inconvenience of doing "proactive parenting"?

2. How can I stay calm when the situation around me is escalating with my child or children? (Some ideas: Deep-breathing 5 times before responding, humming a happy tune to myself, or imagining myself in a safe and calm place, doing something I really enjoy.)

3. Am I willing to STOP talking and calmly act, before I lose my patience?

NOTES

Axiom 3: Give me a healthy diet, and only minimal "dessert", and always after I finish my meals first. I will win if you are inconsistent!

I would try to sneak away from a partially-finished meal and bang on the treat cupboard, but you resisted handing me my dog bone treats and redirected me back to the food bowl. I tried this game many times, but couldn't trick you; guess I caught you when you weren't distracted! Not that I didn't find other ways to try to trick you, like banging on the cupboard when you would be talking on the phone to a friend. When you'd give in to keep me quiet, it just reinforced my doing it again. Talk about behavioral-conditioning (that thing against your ear means I get an extra treat)! Your distraction was my green light! You learned to move with the phone out of the kitchen, so I gave up!

Many of the children I've seen with eating problems over the years existed on very limited, nutritionally-unbalanced diets. There were those children who had sensory issues and found certain textures unpleasant, so needed special counseling to enlarge their willingness to try new foods. Typically, however, those limited diets resulted because children fought for "restaurant-style" meals prepared by parents. Once the "Ugh, I don't like this!" got catered to with an alternative meal, this was the "green light" for children to get negative-attention from harried parents who just wanted a peaceful dinnertime experience!

I've met parents who would even leave the table and take their non-compliant child to the fast-food drive-through, just to get the child to eat something! Beware! This is a set-up for years to come!

WHAT TO DO? At a calm time <u>not</u> centered around eating, share your unhappiness that eating has become an unpleasant experience in your household. Then say the magic words, "SO, FROM NOW ON...." and explain the new family rules about eating: (1) You will provide a few raw veggies/fruits in the middle of the table nightly that your child has eaten in the past (or, are at least, bland, like carrots and celery); (2) You will offer no more than one new food nightly, along with some tried-n-true side dishes; (3) You will expect everyone to take at least a "No, thank you" helping of each food (3 bites). Each child can refuse more if the food is disliked, and substitute raw veggies. If your child won't try any veggies and will only eat the carbohydrate, for example, let him/her finish the serving of it on the plate; (4) If hunger persists, suggest that the rest of the meal on the plate can satisfy that hunger; (5) No seconds until firsts are eaten or tried, as above; (6) If your child is noncompliant, calmly clear the table; and (7) When your child asks for a dessert or later snack, remind him in a nice voice, "Breakfast is the next meal," and casually-mention the choices you are willing to prepare for the next morning. Ignore the drama of your "hungry" child the rest of the evening.

CONCLUSIONS

Pediatricians have assured many parents with whom I've worked that it will not hurt a child to miss a meal or a snack occasionally. YOU, as a parent, need to hold that advice close to your heart, as you, once again, do "proactive parenting." An added test is to do this guilt-free! Remember, that your child's hunger is not imposed by you, but results from a choice your child made at mealtime!

Be prepared for protests, as your child will try to wear you down. If your child typically gets negative-attention for this behavior, things will get worse before they get better! Children will cry harder or protest louder when thwarted, as their desire is to return to old, familiar interactions, rather than face the unknown of new expectations. It takes at least one month to change a habit, and two months to accept it fully! Remember, you are laying the foundation of "normal dietary intake" for a lifetime, as well as positive family interactions at mealtime!

1. Am I willing to stop being a "short order cook" and make one meal a night for my family?

2. Can I learn to tolerate an upset child who has only the choices available on the table to satisfy his/her hunger?

3. What can I do later in the evening when my child complains of hunger and knows that "Breakfast is the next meal"? Am I willing to ride out the protestations in the short run, so as to have peaceful dinnertimes in the long run? Can I tolerate one-to-two months of a "training period"?

NOTES

Axiom 4: When I disobey, teach me what I SHOULD do instead; give me consequences of my behavior calmly.

I LOVED chasing those deer in our yard! After all, it was MY yard and I had to protect it, right? Only trouble was, I'd run right through the electric pet fence, and then be too scared to voluntarily return home back through it. I assume you felt frustrated and worried having to walk the yard's perimeter and find me, while trying to follow my barking. However, you would calmly take off my electric collar, throw it towards home and walk me safely back through the fence. I'd get tied up for a few days if I were left outside, or get "remedial" fence-training, until I learned to just give up and co-exist with the deer on our property!

Babies are innately egocentric! They want their needs met immediately, and will cry instinctively when wet, hungry, tired or hurting. This behavior is self-preserving for our species, as a totally-dependent child's health and growth is best maintained by responsive adults meeting such safety needs.

By age 2 or so, toddlers begin the push for independence, mixed with the continuing need for security. To navigate this stage safely towards self-confidence and continuing independence, children need to learn general "lessons," rather than be punished physically, or with fear-inducing tactics. For example, if a child angrily hits you, empathize with the feeling, but set the limit, while you calmly offer a positive and safe alternative. Then, reinforce the limit again. An example might be: "I see that you are feeling really angry, but I am not for hitting! You can hit the pillow, or your playdough, or throw your nerf ball, but I am not for hitting!" If safe alternatives aren't accepted, proceed with a timeout.

I recall one parent excitedly tell me, after trying the above technique for only two weeks, that she overheard her 4 year-old daughter tell her 2 year-old brother, "Please stop hitting me! People are NOT for hitting!"

CONCLUSIONS

Remember: **Being understood dissipates angry feelings.**

Initially, take a second to empathize with your child's emotion, using the same voice tone and physical reaction (even stomping with matching defiance), as if mirroring your child. This step is typically skipped if a parent thinks the child can be talked into achieving a calmer state. However, when one is in an emotional state, it's very comforting to be TOTALLY understood for one's feelings; action to manage those feelings with practical solutions can come afterwards. It's important to do this mirroring lovingly, so the child does not feel mocked in any way. Then, react to the behavior. You will find that the situation will de-escalate much more smoothly! You'll know you have been successful when the negative-behavior stops, and, especially, when older children repeat the rule to a younger sibling!

This approach really helps with adolescents, too, as it maintains communication during a period which I have nicknamed the "Age of Disdain:" that of rolling eyes, under-the-breath comments and retreating backs. Teens rarely stay emotionally or physically present if they are not feeling heard (which is their typical complaint in counseling sessions). I have convinced many a teen that I hear them by just declaring initially, "Wow! I can see that you REALLY do not want to be here!!" You will be amazed at how quickly a negative relationship with your teen can be turned around by just mirroring feelings first, prior to giving answers! Then, see if a compromise or firm limits are the final result; either way, the outcome will be much calmer if anger is diffused first!

1. How do I feel when an empathic friend or spouse truly listens to an issue I am discussing? Do I like it when the listener just reflects back what I've been saying, without giving me any advice?

2. Do I become calmer when another person truly understands my anger about something?

3. If the discussion stays calm and kind, am I more willing to work to find a solution?

NOTES

Axiom 5: Give me freedom to follow my instincts and grow into the adult I am supposed to become. Praise me when I do a kind act and practice empathy for others!

I was only 3 or 4 years old when I heard you crying from the upstairs bedroom. I came in and saw you on the ground, lying there in pain with a badly-twisted knee. I stayed by your side and barked as loudly as I could, until my Master heard me from the basement and came upstairs and helped you. Finally, I knew what being a "rescue breed" meant! I got lots of extra hugs that day!

Then there was the time when I saw you trying to stop your confused older relative from wandering over to a neighbor's driveway and leaving; she was pushing at you and insisting she needed to continue on! I came running and got in front of her, pressing into her until she stood still and you could redirect her home. You were SO proud of me and even gave me an extra dog biscuit that night!

Emotional intelligence (known as "EQ") has been studied intensively in the past several decades, and found to be a very significant indicator for later success in life. One aspect of EQ is having empathy (a true identification with another's feelings and needs). Children who developed empathy as young as even age two were tracked, and were discovered to become highly popular and academically-successful, as well as school leaders. Those with such characteristics possess a precursor for job success, as empathic leaders tend to tune into personal, as well as professional concerns, of others, and, thus, foster willing cooperation from their co-workers.

Human beings also have a natural desire to evolve and mature. No one wishes to "stay stuck;" so, it is normal for children to strive for increasing independence. Young children are like sponges as they are evolving: They absorb everything in their environment! Once children have added positive or negative concepts and role-modeling to their repertoire of beliefs and actions, it is hard to dissuade them of their new-found knowledge. Therefore, it is helpful to instill the positive in children from the start, as well as practice it between spouses, who are under their children's acute observation!

We are basically social beings and want to connect. It is imperative for parents to role-model for their young children ways to act civically and morally- responsible. Young children can donate to food banks, give old toys to needy children, save their pennies for the less fortunate, read to and visit elderly relatives or neighbors, help you fill a backpack for a needy schoolchild, or help as you pick a family to provide for at Christmas, to give just a few ideas.

In your daily life, notice when your child plays kindly, spontaneously helps a sibling or peer, or does a chore graciously without being reminded. A simple comment such as, "I'm happy to see the two of you laughing and enjoying playing that game together," or "thank you for helping your sister tie her shoe", creates a positive atmosphere.

CONCLUSION

Catch your child being responsible.

Children love praise and will rise to the occasion again, if they know their previous actions have pleased you. Continued positive reinforcement by you will do wonders!

Never do for your child what he can do for himself. Help make clothes and school supplies reachable on low hangars or hooks. Make a snack chart together and post it on the refrigerator; imagine not having to negotiate each day after school what snacks are permitted! Commend your child on his increasing independence and self-confidence.

When you are frustrated with a predominant trait your child is exhibiting, such as "stubbornness," reframe it! Say, "Wow! You are a very determined person! You don't give up easily; that will be very helpful to you when you are older!" Such reframing will also help you to see your child in a new, more positive light.

Remember, "Goodwill creates goodwill!

1. How do I role-model showing empathy to others?

2. What family activities do I do with my children to encourage their social awareness of other persons' needs?

3. How do my children know when I am proud of their spontaneous kindness to others?

NOTES

Axiom 6: Teach me to socialize gently and slowly, without overdoing it or pressuring me.

You encouraged me to lay down submissively when smaller dogs or little children came near, which allowed them to come close and investigate me before I responded in kind. After all, my size could frighten others, if this were a first encounter! You then let me interact at my pace and I became a big hit with everyone!

When a "guest" dog wanted my toys, or my food or treats, you encouraged me to share them willingly. If I had enough "sharing," a gentle growl helped me reassert myself as hosting dog of the house, and you respected that I had enough sharing for the day!

A shy child typically feels the pressure from "support" people to talk and play with peers, whether ready or not. Often, if contact with the child is minimal after the initial greeting period, the child will edge forward and investigate the action at his/her own pace. All forward movement then becomes a success, rather than judged in any way as "not good enough."

It is critical, however, to teach a shy child how to avoid being a "victim" of another aggressive or overbearing child. Teach this child to loudly state, "I don't like that! Please stop!" You can playfully have yelling contests using these words at home, until the quiet child finds a voice. Encourage this assertive approach first, and then, telling a grownup if that isn't enough.

Contract with your child, if there is a request to join a new sport or start another activity, to "stay the season." Stay low-key about performance, and focus instead on the potential fun, exercise, learning experience and camaraderie the activity may provide. For piano or other lessons, contract for a year, and provide the time and encouragement for regular practice at home, even if the practice becomes tedious. Children need to learn the concept of "delayed gratification" in achieving new skill-levels, and are typically proud of their ensuing achievements.

Teach your child this:

"With every new thing you try to do,

You'll feel more confident about your whole world, too!"

Risk-taking is necessary to conquer anxiety. Give your children examples of how you conquered anxious moments as a child. Expose your children to all kinds of activities, situations, and experiences, while letting them absorb the learning at their own pace. A light of interest may go on when you least expect it, but children need the exposure to stimulate that interest. One friend's child struggled learning to ride a bike, but finally decided to ask a friend to help him, so he could occasionally interact socially in a neighborhood full of bike-riding peers. He preferred to spend the rest of his spare time finding "critters" in the creek, and is now a marine biologist!

If a tried-activity does not mesh well with your child, for whatever reason, encourage your child to try other new experiences until he/she finds a fit. Commend your child for trying something new and provide reassurance that the world needs all kinds of people, who can do all kinds of things!

1. If you have a shy child, which parent can most identify with those feelings from their own childhood? How can you normalize social concerns for your child?

2. Can you tolerate your child acting timid in a social gathering? What if other people comment negatively about such behavior? How can YOU act assertively with these people?

3. Are you willing to explain that any new activity, especially team sports or expensive instrument or art lessons, creates a minimum time commitment if pursued by your child? Would a written contract be helpful before beginning the activity?

4. Are you willing to help your child problem-solve small issues initially and then try to resolve them alone? If you need to speak with a teacher or a neighbor's child and parent about an issue, are you willing to ask your child first if he or she would like to be present? (Of course, this is dependent on your child's age and the severity of the situation.)

NOTES

Axiom 7: Please notice me when I want or need extra attention or loving.

Sometimes, I was perfectly content to nap on my own, in another room. At other times, I wanted to be "glued" to your side as you moved around the house, even showing separation-anxiety by getting up and moving to the new spot, if you were temporarily out-of-sight. When you would settle on to the couch to read or watch television, I would come lay down by your feet, and "paw" your foot to be petted. It became a silly game at times, to watch me "reawaken" if you stopped the rhythmic petting.

It might take a few seconds, but I always "re-pawed" you for more. Finally, when you wanted to stop playing, you would tell me so in a kind but firm, no-nonsense voice, and I would give in and lay back down, having gotten a long dose of your attention!

Children need to trust that when they need a hug, or a loved one to listen to an important discussion (at least, important to THEM), that they will be noticed and heard. They also need to accept occasional delays in receiving immediate gratification, as other people may be in the midst of something that can't be put off right then. The key is to find the balance between the two extremes of responding quickly every time, versus delaying quickly every time!

I encourage you to begin a daily, ten-minute "Just Us Time" with your child. Initially, explain the parameters of the activity to your child. (1) Make it separate from bedtime rituals, (2) Meet the same time of day, (3) Start at the same place (a spot your child gets to pick), and, most importantly, (4) Insist that your child choose the conversation or activity. (5) Then, remind your child JUST ONCE ten minutes before, start a timer, and show up at the designated place ten minutes later. (6) If your child forgets, or chooses not to meet with you, then leave at the end of the period and go about your day. (7) Also, reset the timer when you begin, and stop the activity when the timer goes off! It is difficult to maintain elongated periods every day, but ten minutes is typically manageable. (8) If an activity or game is unfinished, and your child wishes to continue it the next day, see if there is a space to leave it out.

If you are in the midst of making dinner, etc., and your child wants you to play a game or do an activity, you can thus say, "I need to finish dinner right now, but you can choose to do that at our "Just Us Time" later....

Make sure other siblings do not intervene in another child's time. In fact, if the other parent can do a "Just Us Time" with the sibling and then switch, this is even better! If you have several children, you may have to do opposite nights to get everyone a turn at least several times weekly.

Focus totally on your child when you can, and set attention-limits only when it is truly necessary.

Remember to try the "Just Us Time" technique. I've never seen a child refuse it! I've even seen older teenagers enjoy painting or weight-lifting with a parent, or just talking together. Bedtime "delays" are often a quest for private time with a parent; saturating that need earlier each evening will make the bedtime routine go much smoother. It's amazing, but you will see negative attention-seeking diminish within a few weeks, once your child is convinced that he/she will have your undivided attention for at least those ten minutes daily! If you are going to be away, let your child know, and try to reschedule "Just Us Time" together, or coordinate a phone call or webcam at that time period.

We all need to feel special and unique at times; this enables us to happily "pay it forward."

1. Are you willing to try this "Just Us Time" for a month, before drawing conclusions about its helpfulness?

2. Can you avoid offering ideas for how to spend the time, even if your child says, "I don't know what to do!"? (Practice saying, "It's your time; I'm sure you can decide...")

3. What would it be like to delay a request for attention when you are truly preoccupied, and know you have a private time set apart for later in the day?

NOTES

Axiom 8: Take time to be extra kind when you need to leave me behind.

You and my Master used to travel just a little bit when I was young, and you usually brought one of your grown-up friends to the house to stay with me while you were gone. I got lots of walks, petting, treats, and attention. Sometimes, you would call home and my dog sitter would let me come near the phone to hear your voice.

When I was older, and you both were able to take longer trips, you left me at "that dog place," so that I could socialize with friends. I missed you a lot! It helped that you'd give the owners my special bed, my stuffed monkey, all my medicines, and the advice to give me some broth on my dry food if I didn't feel as hungry because I was missing you. After awhile, those people became friends, too! I loved playing "keep-away" with them outside during playtime; the people told you how much I would make them laugh!

Children like routine and struggle when changes are impending in their lives, as when a parent has to work late often, or if parents take a trip and leave them with a sitter or relative. Small children struggle to visualize where you are staying when you are out-of-sight.

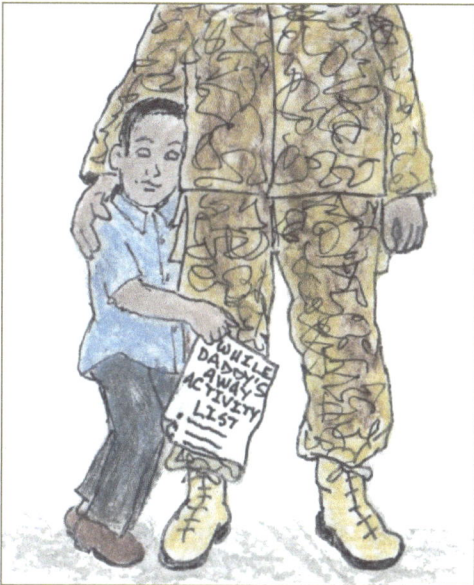

There are so many ways to alleviate the abandonment they naturally feel! If you can take your children to your workplace, this will help them later to understand where you are and what you are doing when away. Before travelling, show your children what your motel, location or activity is going to look like. You can go online, or leave them a brochure; this will also help ground your children during your absence.

For very young children, create and decorate a "clothesline" together of separate sheets of paper with a number on each, that count off the number of days you will be gone. Each evening, your child can take down a number and visually see the remaining days.

You can leave little notes and small, inexpensive surprises for them daily while you are gone. The notes can engage you with what the child's activities are for that particular day (i.e., ""Have fun at dance class tonight! Your Grandma will be glad to help you get your tap shoes on, I'm sure!")

You can read a story into a tape player, and then give your child the book and tape for the first night you will be gone. The caregiver can read the story once with your child, or let your child turn the pages alone and listen to your voice reading the story. This often helps as a transition to sleep, if the limit is that the story can be listened to once more after the caregiver leaves the room.

With today's cellular phones, computers and webcams, pre-arranged "visits" can be done daily. Or, you might even surprise your child by leaving written clues for a "treasure hunt" of a memento you've tucked away somewhere in the house or in the yard.

It is normal for young children to initially act stand-offish upon your return as a way to show their displeasure for you leaving them. Allow this phase to dissipate naturally; and your youngsters will soon want to share their adventures of the week and learn about yours!

CONCLUSIONS

Understand the expected feelings of abandonment in your children, provide empathy and affection, and then casually move forward with your plans.

Try to prepare your child for your absence with tangible examples of where you will be. Provide thoughtful gestures to let your children know you are thinking of them in your absence and will be excited to see them upon your return.

For very young children, create a visual and tactile activity together that can count off the days until your return.

Allow a "warm-up period" upon your return. Bringing home a surprise helps bridge the gap, also!

1. Do your children have a visual recall or sense of where you are when you are away? How might you help them understand even better? Have they seen your workplace?

2. What regular activities do your children participate in that you can "join in with" long-distance? Can you mark these on your work calendar before your trip each time?

3. What fun activity/small present/set of loving notes can you leave behind? What "countdown" activity can you create to help clarify the longevity of your absence?

NOTES

Axiom 9: Please help me when I am helpless.

I tried my best to carry on self-sufficiently when I would cut my paw, or itch from bug bites. You would intervene when you thought you could make me more comfortable. The trust built up between us over the years assured me that you would always act as my "safety person" so I calmly accepted any first aid or soothing you would provide to me. I really loved your hugs and soft words, too!

When I no longer could use my back legs, and all the testing showed spinal deterioration, you did all you could to make me more pain-free. When I failed to rally again as I had done the year before, you decided to let me go, as my peace was more important to you, than your sadness over saying good-by to me.

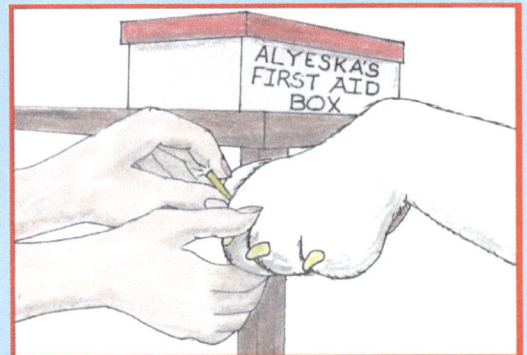

Children need to gain independence, but first need to know that you are there to provide medical first-aid, hugs and kisses to soothe "hurties," and emotional and physical support when they are bullied, traumatized, or frightened.

Take their concerns seriously, and do not attempt to minimize them (i.e., "There aren't any monsters in your room! Don't be such a baby!"). Instead, help THEM strategize how to regain control over their fears. A great help for "monsters" can be handmade (or computer-generated) "Monster-Free Zone" signs for a child's room, done as a poster, or with the scariest monster your child can draw, with a circle and crossed-through line over it. You can also make up "Grandma's Secret Monster-Scaring Potion" (with recipe passed on from your childhood, once you are a mom); use your imagination here! It can just be water with magical, soundless words said over it, or can be "secretly" made up in another room. Let your child spray it wherever the feared monsters might take up residence!

The key is to comfort first, and then empower second. Another example is if your child becomes afraid of blood or injuries, after experiencing one herself/himself. You can create a "first aid drawer" in the kitchen or bathroom within your child's reach. Make your child in charge, under your supervision, of washing, patting dry, applying antiseptic and adding a bandage to family members' simple cuts and scratches. This will empower your child and usually alleviate the fear of blood.

A repeated theme I have observed throughout my child counseling career is that past incidents can prove to be a "Big Trauma" or a "little trauma." What might seem like an insignificant situation to a parent may loom as a Big Trauma, or core hurt, in your child's life. I recall once how a teacher didn't believe a screaming student had a bee buzzing in her ear that had flown in through the open classroom window. The teacher told the child to "not be so dramatic and make up lies." That child carried the negative belief "I cannot be trusted" into adulthood, and it continued to affect her until she healed the origins of that erroneous belief.

CONCLUSIONS

When a child feels secure and safe, then natural resilience will enable your child to adapt to minor or major trauma with a "can-do" attitude and fewer repercussions.

Be open-minded about evaluating how serious an incident is to your child; do not assume the incident is insignificant unless your child also appears nonplussed by it. You may also observe a very delayed-reaction about a prior incident if your child is triggered by a similar incident in the future. Just consider if anything in the past could be fueling a child's reaction to what seems to be a very minor current situation; i.e., put on your "detective" hat!

If a child feels emotionally-threatened, listen seriously to the story, ask how the child feels about it, and then discuss ways to problem-solve the issue. Ask your child if he or she would like to try to work through the problem first, without any other help from you. If so, check in afterwards to see if the child's own efforts worked. Intervene to speak with other adult authority figures only when the problem is out of your child's control to further resolve.

1. How do I help my child handle their fears calmly? Can I put them in charge of conquering fears with some concrete ideas?

2. If my child gets hurt, do I stay calm so that my child feels reassured of my competence to help take care of the injury?

3. How can I listen more patiently and thoroughly to my child to determine if a prior incident could be aggravating my child's reaction to a current situation?

NOTES

Axiom 10: Continue to love others the way you loved me. I know you have plenty of love to go around.

You know you can love other peoples' pets, because I have filled your heart with enough love to keep sharing it. Please share my belongings with special pets in your life, but keep one or two special items for mementos of our time together. Tell your loved ones stories about our adventures, as I know you will gain comfort from doing so. I am so glad that I helped affirm for you, by our special bond, that "what goes around comes around." I am proud to remain, always, your "sweet Aly Girl."

Role-modeling love and consideration for others, even strangers you meet, shows your children how to "get back more than they give." Teaching your children how to find the goodness in all people, the nuggets of wisdom each person we encounter can give us, and how to put others first in their lives, can give them the confidence and kind demeanor that will make our children socially-appreciated and respected by others.

When dealing with the loss of a loved one, if a child can be helped to compile a "memory album," or maintain a tradition the loved one valued (a cherished holiday recipe, a favorite craft, an altruistic activity), the healing can occur more easily, as the child can keep the deceased person in his/her heart more readily. An example might be, if Grandma used to volunteer monthly at the homeless shelter, can you and your child send cookies to the shelter in her memory?

If your child is struggling with the inability to "talk to Grandma," you can have the child write Grandma a letter, fold it into a helium balloon, and release it together into the sky. This technique has proven very empowering for many children. Just bring the note to the store and ask to have it enclosed, before the balloon is blown up.

In addition, I have noticed many children going through strong feelings of loss when a best friend moves away, whether as a military child, a child of divorcing parents, or due to general parental job changes. Also, children can feel loss "graduating" from one grade to another, especially if a prior favorite teacher is replaced by a less-liked teacher. Changing schools due to one's own move can also create a strong grief reaction in a child. It can be helpful to revisit the former school and friends at winter break or the next summer. By then, your child will probably have moved on enough to prefer a return to the new friends and surroundings.

Sometimes, the pain of a pet's death from earlier years can be triggered by a new loss of a person, or vice-versa. Search your mind for previous losses, even seemingly-small ones, if your child shows signs of depression. Acknowledge other former losses verbally with your child.

Please consider short-term counseling for your child if grief continues to impact your child's daily life to the point of personality change or withdrawal from daily activities. Honor your gut feeling that healing is not proceeding at a manageable-rate on its own.

CONCLUSIONS

Children are typically very resilient, and attention to their grief over a loss can help tremendously to shorten the healing process.

It is normal to take up to two years to heal from the loss of a beloved relative or pet. Many children I have seen speak for years about missing their pets, especially, because these animals were present in their daily lives even more than a distant relative may have been. Also, the "size" of a pet (i.e., a hermit crab or a goldfish, versus a dog or cat) is not necessarily proportional to the size of a child's grief about losing it.

Please do not rush out to quickly replace a recently-deceased pet. Give your child several months to process the loss first. Also, while focused on healing your child's grief, don't forget to deal with your own, both for yourself and as a role-model for your child.

1. What losses have I or my child sustained in the last several years that might still be upsetting my child?

2. Has my child been sad about a friend moving or graduating? What about my own child changing grades and missing a teacher?

3. Have my family's circumstances changed recently? (This could include parental separation or divorce, deployment of a parent, illness of another relative, a job loss, etc.)

4. What rituals do we have in place as a family to help with grief? What might we institute?

NOTES

Summary

AXIOM	CONCLUSIONS
1. Remember the unadulterated glee of that first moment you laid eyes on me.	When upset, keep IN sight your memory of your FIRST sight of me!
2. Enjoy my playful behavior, while setting limits to rein me in safely.	Consistency, consistency, consistency is the key.
3. Give me a healthy diet, and only minimal "dessert," and always after I finish my meals first. I will win if you are inconsistent!	Maintain a guilt-free, nonchalant attitude about eating. Children will eat what's available when alternatives aren't there.
4. When I disobey, teach me what I SHOULD do instead. Give me the consequences of my behavior calmly.	Criticize the ACTION, not the child. Provide a time for your child to "regroup." Teach positive options.
5. Give me freedom to follow my instincts and grow into the adult I'm supposed to become. Praise me when I do a kind act and practice empathy for others!	Give your child space and opportunity to mature independently. Concentrate on the development of your child's Emotional Intelligence.
6. Teach me to socialize gently and slowly, without overdoing it or pressuring me.	Develop the individuality of your child. Praise his attempts to overcome his limitations.
7. Please notice me when I want or need extra attention or loving.	Replace negative attention-seeking with regular positive time together.
8. Take time to be extra kind when you leave me behind.	Understand a child's need for consistent attachment and leave reminders of your love around.
9. Please help me when I am helpless.	Keep first-aid calm and nonchalant. Praise attempts at self-sufficiency.
10. Continue to love others the way you loved me. I know you have plenty of love to go around.	Provide concrete ways to remember and celebrate a lost loved one. Help your child share love with others.

About The Author

Joyce Meagher graduated with a BS in Nursing from the University of Michigan. She moved throughout the United States as a military wife for 21 years, while raising 2 children, plus several dogs, cats, guinea pigs, gerbils, and birds. Joyce received her MA in Counseling from Wright State University in Ohio and began her specialization in child play therapy in 1978. She continues in her private practice in Fairfax, VA, seeing all clients of all ages, while teaching and mentoring counseling and play therapy students.

Joyce's illustrator/husband, Jim, is a "man of many talents." Hopefully, this is just the first Alyeska story; a future series of her playful adventures will need Jim's artistic hand again!

Ordering Books

$19 each ($18 each for 2 or more books) Add $5.00 S&H per book in USA (1-2 week delivery)
VA Residents: Add 5% sales tax per book

More than 10 Books or International Orders – Send email to kdknzlr@comcast.net with your request details

Send check or money order to:
LifeSpan Counseling
6204 Sierra Ct
Manassas, VA 20111 USA

Order form available at http://www.jmmcounseling.com